This book is dedicated with love to:

Our parents
Regina and Edward Dowgiallo
Constance and Charles Schulze

Our children
Dawn and Bobby

Our grandchildren
Alexander and Meghan

In Memory of
John P. Farrelly

The authors wish to sincerely thank the following,
without whom this book would not be possible:

The Carmelite Sisters
of the Most Sacred Heart of Los Angeles
(the artwork in this book is based on their original drawings)

Brother Denis Sennett, S.A.

Marian Caputo

Sister Beth Anne Herrmann, O.S.F.

Father Leonard DiFalco

On that first Christmas Eve,
There was peace o'er the land.

Date

_____

This book belongs to

_____

Given by

_____

On That First Christmas Eve...

Carol Schulze Dowgiallo & Robert Dowgiallo

Illustrated by Dorothy Perez

Our Sunday Visitor Publishing Division
Our Sunday Visitor, Inc.
Huntington, Indiana 46750

Nihil Obstat: Rev. Michael Heintz
Censor Librorum

Imprimatur: ✠ John M. D'Arcy
Bishop of Fort Wayne-South Bend
June 5, 2005

Our Sunday Visitor Publishing Division
Our Sunday Visitor, Inc.
200 Noll Plaza
Huntington, IN 46750

ISBN: 1-59276-183-6 (Inventory No. T234)

Cover design by Troy Lefevra
Cover and interior art by Dorothy Perez
Interior design by Sherri L. Hoffman

PRINTED IN KOREA

But heaven was stirring;
Great events were at hand.

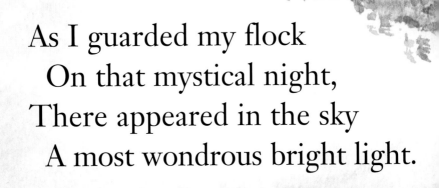

As I guarded my flock
  On that mystical night,
There appeared in the sky
  A most wondrous bright light.

8

'Twas an angel of God,
And he pointed the way

To Bethlehem's manger,
To the crib filled with hay.

He said to me calmly,
 "There's no need to fear,
For God's Son will be born
As morning draws near."

So to David's town
I ran as fast as I could,

Over meadow and hillside,
Through pasture and wood.

Once reaching the manger,
It was unclear to me
How this one little child
Could change history.

There in that small crib,
The infant Jesus lay,
So peaceful, so quiet,
Asleep on the hay.

God's Word was made flesh,
  Just as the angel had told,
Good Shepherd of mankind,
  But a few hours old.

His most loving parents
  Knelt by Him in prayer;
Mary and Joseph
  Would always be there.

This started for Mary
    When she gladly said "Yes"
To the angel who told her
    She truly was blest.

But deep in her heart
I could tell Mary knew,
What the prophets foretold
Must someday come true.

Visiting wise men
  Came from afar,
Bearing gifts to the manger,
  Led by a bright star.

To avoid Herod's wrath,
  The Holy Family would go;
Returning to Nazareth,
  Young Jesus would grow.

Baptized in the waters
    Of the Jordan one day,
He would constantly teach us
    Our Father's good way.

Giving food to the hungry,
And aid to the poor,
We must do in His name,
And, oh, so much more!

Always loving and serving
Our God above all,
Forgiving our neighbor
As ourselves was His call.

He made the lame walk,
  Gave sight to the blind,
Cured all people's illness,
  Both body and mind.

Jesus preached of His kingdom
  That someday will be
When all those held captive
  Are finally set free.

But then came that time,
  The most Holy Week,
The Passover Feast,
  When His death they did seek.

Jesus' Body and Blood
    On Holy Thursday He gave,
This Sacrifice offered
    So that all He would save.

Led to Mount Calvary,
To be nailed to the cross,
Jesus lay in the tomb,
And all hope seemed a loss.

If events ended there,
    We would all be forlorn,
But a miracle took place
That first Easter morn.

Rising from the dead,
  Seen by each faithful friend,
He proved to us all
  That our lives have no end.

Ascending to heaven,
  To His Father He went,
And as He had promised,
  The Holy Spirit He sent:

To gently guide us along,
  Through good times and strife,
Our comfort and our strength,
  All the days of this life.

But back to that night,
  To that first Christmas Eve,
When God's greatest gift,
  His only Son we receive.

As I knelt by that crib,
  Filled with wonder and glee,

The meaning of this night
Now became clear to me.

Many angels appeared
  In that heavenly sky,
A most radiant host
  Praising God from on high.

And they sang out as one,
  A glorious amen:
"May there be peace on earth,
  And goodwill towards all men."

About the Authors

Carol and Robert Dowgiallo own and operate a company that provides practice-management software and training for the medical profession. They are the parents of two grown children, Dawn and Bobby. Their two beautiful grandchildren, Alexander and Meghan, have inspired Carol and Robert to discover anew the true meaning of Christmas and to collaborate on the writing of *On That First Christmas Eve*, which they describe as a "labor of love." This is their first book.

About the Illustrator

Dorothy Perez is the mother of three wonderful children: Aaron, Lucas, and Maria. She holds a bachelor's degree in communications design from Kutztown University, Pennsylvania, and is the illustrator of *Catholic Cardlinks: Prayers* (Our Sunday Visitor). Dorothy thanks her husband, Luis, and her children "for allowing me the time to work on this wonderful book," and she adds: "I enjoy illustrating because it allows me to marry my faith with the talent that God gave me."